50 Fun and Flavorful Fusion Tacos Recipes

By: Kelly Johnson

Table of Contents

- Korean BBQ Beef Tacos
- Thai Chicken Tacos with Peanut Sauce
- Mediterranean Lamb Tacos with Tzatziki
- Buffalo Cauliflower Tacos with Blue Cheese
- Jamaican Jerk Chicken Tacos
- Vietnamese Pork Tacos with Pickled Veggies
- Indian Spiced Chickpea Tacos
- Moroccan Lamb Tacos with Harissa
- Hawaiian Poke Tacos
- Chipotle Shrimp Tacos with Avocado Cream
- BBQ Pulled Pork Tacos with Pineapple Salsa
- Greek Chicken Tacos with Feta and Olives
- Italian Sausage and Peppers Tacos
- Spicy Miso Fish Tacos
- Sweet and Sour Tofu Tacos
- Banh Mi Tacos with Pork and Pickled Carrots
- Southern Fried Chicken Tacos
- Peruvian Chicken Tacos with Aji Verde
- Cajun Shrimp Tacos with Remoulade
- Tex-Mex Breakfast Tacos with Chorizo
- German Bratwurst Tacos with Sauerkraut
- Ramen Noodle Tacos with Pork Belly
- Spanish Chorizo and Egg Tacos
- Pesto Chicken Tacos with Mozzarella
- Crab and Avocado Tacos with Cilantro Lime Dressing
- Filipino Adobo Chicken Tacos
- Vegan Jackfruit Tacos with Mango Salsa
- Swedish Meatball Tacos with Lingonberry Sauce
- Szechuan Beef Tacos with Cabbage Slaw
- Cilantro Lime Grilled Shrimp Tacos
- Smoked Salmon Tacos with Cream Cheese and Capers
- Eggplant Parmesan Tacos
- Maple Glazed Salmon Tacos with Slaw
- Coconut Curry Chicken Tacos
- Thai Red Curry Shrimp Tacos

- Chili Lime Mango Chicken Tacos
- Ratatouille Veggie Tacos
- Buffalo Chicken Tacos with Ranch Dressing
- Tandoori Chicken Tacos with Mint Yogurt
- Fajita-style Beef Tacos with Chimichurri
- Lemon Herb Grilled Chicken Tacos
- Sriracha Tofu Tacos with Sesame Slaw
- Curried Beef Tacos with Raita
- Cilantro Lime Pork Tacos with Avocado
- Grilled Veggie Tacos with Balsamic Glaze
- Egg and Bacon Breakfast Tacos
- Spicy Tuna Poke Tacos
- Roasted Vegetable Tacos with Hummus
- Balsamic Chicken Tacos with Goat Cheese
- Lobster Tacos with Cilantro and Lime

Korean BBQ Beef Tacos

Ingredients:

- 1 lb beef (flank or sirloin), thinly sliced
- 1/4 cup soy sauce
- 2 tbsp brown sugar
- 1 tbsp sesame oil
- 2 cloves garlic, minced
- 1 tsp ginger, minced
- Corn or flour tortillas
- Toppings: sliced green onions, cilantro, kimchi, sesame seeds

Instructions:

1. In a bowl, combine soy sauce, brown sugar, sesame oil, garlic, and ginger. Marinate the beef in this mixture for at least 30 minutes.
2. Heat a grill or skillet over medium-high heat. Cook the marinated beef for 3-4 minutes until cooked through.
3. Warm the tortillas. Assemble tacos with beef and desired toppings. Serve immediately.

Thai Chicken Tacos with Peanut Sauce

Ingredients:

- 2 cups cooked chicken, shredded
- 1/4 cup peanut butter
- 2 tbsp soy sauce
- 1 tbsp lime juice
- 1 tbsp honey
- Corn or flour tortillas
- Toppings: shredded cabbage, carrots, cilantro

Instructions:

1. In a small bowl, mix peanut butter, soy sauce, lime juice, and honey to make the peanut sauce.
2. In a separate bowl, combine shredded chicken with half of the peanut sauce.
3. Warm the tortillas and fill with the chicken mixture. Top with shredded cabbage, carrots, and cilantro. Drizzle with more peanut sauce before serving.

Mediterranean Lamb Tacos with Tzatziki

Ingredients:

- 1 lb ground lamb
- 1 tsp cumin
- 1 tsp coriander
- Salt and pepper to taste
- Corn or flour tortillas
- Toppings: diced tomatoes, red onion, fresh parsley
- For Tzatziki: 1 cup Greek yogurt, 1 cucumber (grated), 1 clove garlic (minced), 1 tbsp lemon juice, salt to taste

Instructions:

1. In a skillet, cook ground lamb with cumin, coriander, salt, and pepper until browned and cooked through.
2. In a bowl, mix Greek yogurt, grated cucumber, garlic, lemon juice, and salt to make the tzatziki sauce.
3. Warm the tortillas and fill with lamb, then top with diced tomatoes, red onion, parsley, and a drizzle of tzatziki.

Buffalo Cauliflower Tacos with Blue Cheese

Ingredients:

- 1 head cauliflower, cut into florets
- 1/2 cup buffalo sauce
- Corn or flour tortillas
- Toppings: crumbled blue cheese, celery, ranch dressing

Instructions:

1. Preheat the oven to 425°F (220°C). Toss cauliflower florets with buffalo sauce and spread on a baking sheet.
2. Bake for 25-30 minutes until crispy.
3. Warm the tortillas and fill with roasted cauliflower. Top with blue cheese, celery, and ranch dressing.

Jamaican Jerk Chicken Tacos

Ingredients:

- 1 lb chicken thighs, boneless and skinless
- 2 tbsp jerk seasoning
- Corn or flour tortillas
- Toppings: mango salsa, cilantro, lime wedges

Instructions:

1. Rub jerk seasoning all over chicken thighs and let marinate for at least 30 minutes.
2. Grill or sauté chicken until cooked through (about 5-7 minutes per side).
3. Warm the tortillas and fill with sliced chicken. Top with mango salsa and cilantro. Serve with lime wedges.

Vietnamese Pork Tacos with Pickled Veggies

Ingredients:

- 1 lb pork shoulder, thinly sliced
- 1 tbsp soy sauce
- 1 tbsp fish sauce
- 1 tbsp sugar
- Corn or flour tortillas
- Pickled veggies (carrots, daikon, and cucumbers)
- Toppings: fresh cilantro, sliced jalapeños

Instructions:

1. Marinate the pork in soy sauce, fish sauce, and sugar for 30 minutes.
2. In a skillet, cook the pork over medium-high heat until cooked through.
3. Warm the tortillas and fill with pork, then top with pickled veggies, cilantro, and jalapeños.

Indian Spiced Chickpea Tacos

Ingredients:

- 1 can (15 oz) chickpeas, drained and rinsed
- 1 tbsp curry powder
- 1 tsp cumin
- Corn or flour tortillas
- Toppings: diced tomatoes, red onion, cilantro, yogurt

Instructions:

1. In a skillet, sauté chickpeas with curry powder, cumin, salt, and pepper until heated through.
2. Warm the tortillas and fill with spiced chickpeas. Top with diced tomatoes, red onion, cilantro, and a dollop of yogurt.

Moroccan Lamb Tacos with Harissa

Ingredients:

- 1 lb ground lamb
- 1 tsp cinnamon
- 1 tsp cumin
- 1 tsp paprika
- Salt and pepper to taste
- Corn or flour tortillas
- Toppings: harissa sauce, diced cucumbers, mint

Instructions:

1. In a skillet, cook ground lamb with cinnamon, cumin, paprika, salt, and pepper until browned.
2. Warm the tortillas and fill with lamb. Top with harissa, diced cucumbers, and mint. Serve warm.

Hawaiian Poke Tacos

Ingredients:

- 1 lb sushi-grade tuna, diced
- 1/4 cup soy sauce
- 1 tbsp sesame oil
- 1 avocado, diced
- Corn or flour tortillas
- Toppings: sliced green onions, sesame seeds, seaweed salad

Instructions:

1. In a bowl, mix diced tuna with soy sauce and sesame oil. Let marinate for about 10 minutes.
2. Warm the tortillas and fill with marinated tuna.
3. Top with avocado, sliced green onions, sesame seeds, and seaweed salad. Serve immediately.

Chipotle Shrimp Tacos with Avocado Cream

Ingredients:

- 1 lb shrimp, peeled and deveined
- 2 tbsp chipotle sauce
- 1 avocado
- 1/4 cup sour cream
- Corn or flour tortillas
- Toppings: cabbage slaw, lime wedges

Instructions:

1. In a bowl, toss shrimp with chipotle sauce. Cook in a skillet over medium heat until pink and cooked through (about 3-4 minutes).
2. In a blender, combine avocado, sour cream, and a pinch of salt until smooth to make the avocado cream.
3. Warm the tortillas and fill with shrimp. Top with cabbage slaw and a drizzle of avocado cream. Serve with lime wedges.

BBQ Pulled Pork Tacos with Pineapple Salsa

Ingredients:

- 2 cups cooked pulled pork
- 1/2 cup BBQ sauce
- Corn or flour tortillas
- Pineapple salsa (1 cup diced pineapple, 1/4 cup red onion, 1/4 cup cilantro, juice of 1 lime)

Instructions:

1. In a saucepan, combine pulled pork with BBQ sauce and heat until warm.
2. To make the pineapple salsa, mix diced pineapple, red onion, cilantro, and lime juice in a bowl.
3. Warm the tortillas and fill with BBQ pulled pork. Top with pineapple salsa and serve warm.

Greek Chicken Tacos with Feta and Olives

Ingredients:

- 1 lb chicken breast, grilled and sliced
- 1/2 cup Greek yogurt
- 1/4 cup feta cheese, crumbled
- Corn or flour tortillas
- Toppings: sliced olives, diced tomatoes, cucumber

Instructions:

1. Warm the tortillas and fill with sliced grilled chicken.
2. Top with Greek yogurt, crumbled feta, sliced olives, diced tomatoes, and cucumber. Serve warm.

Italian Sausage and Peppers Tacos

Ingredients:

- 1 lb Italian sausage (sweet or spicy)
- 1 bell pepper, sliced
- 1 onion, sliced
- Corn or flour tortillas
- Toppings: grated Parmesan cheese, fresh basil

Instructions:

1. In a skillet, cook Italian sausage until browned. Remove and slice. In the same skillet, sauté bell pepper and onion until softened.
2. Warm the tortillas and fill with sausage, sautéed peppers, and onions.
3. Top with grated Parmesan cheese and fresh basil. Serve warm.

Spicy Miso Fish Tacos

Ingredients:

- 1 lb white fish (like cod or tilapia)
- 2 tbsp miso paste
- 1 tbsp sriracha
- Corn or flour tortillas
- Toppings: cabbage slaw, cilantro, lime wedges

Instructions:

1. Mix miso paste and sriracha. Spread the mixture over the fish and grill or bake until cooked through (about 10-12 minutes).
2. Warm the tortillas and fill with cooked fish.
3. Top with cabbage slaw and cilantro. Serve with lime wedges.

Sweet and Sour Tofu Tacos

Ingredients:

- 1 block firm tofu, cubed
- 1/4 cup sweet and sour sauce
- Corn or flour tortillas
- Toppings: diced bell peppers, green onions

Instructions:

1. In a skillet, sauté cubed tofu until golden. Add sweet and sour sauce and cook until heated through.
2. Warm the tortillas and fill with sweet and sour tofu.
3. Top with diced bell peppers and green onions. Serve warm.

Banh Mi Tacos with Pork and Pickled Carrots

Ingredients:

- 1 lb pork tenderloin, cooked and sliced
- 1/2 cup pickled carrots (carrots pickled in vinegar, sugar, and salt)
- Corn or flour tortillas
- Toppings: sliced cucumbers, fresh cilantro, jalapeños

Instructions:

1. Warm the tortillas and fill with sliced pork.
2. Top with pickled carrots, sliced cucumbers, cilantro, and jalapeños. Serve warm.

Southern Fried Chicken Tacos

Ingredients:

- 1 lb fried chicken tenders, chopped
- Corn or flour tortillas
- Toppings: coleslaw, pickles, hot sauce

Instructions:

1. Warm the tortillas and fill with chopped fried chicken.
2. Top with coleslaw, pickles, and a drizzle of hot sauce. Serve warm.

Peruvian Chicken Tacos with Aji Verde

Ingredients:

- 1 lb cooked chicken, shredded
- Corn or flour tortillas
- **Aji Verde Sauce:**
    - 1 cup cilantro
    - 1 jalapeño, seeded
    - 2 cloves garlic
    - 1/2 cup mayonnaise
    - 1 tbsp lime juice
    - Salt to taste

Instructions:

1. In a blender, combine cilantro, jalapeño, garlic, mayonnaise, lime juice, and salt. Blend until smooth to make the aji verde sauce.
2. Warm the tortillas and fill with shredded chicken.
3. Drizzle with aji verde sauce and serve warm.

Cajun Shrimp Tacos with Remoulade

Ingredients:

- 1 lb shrimp, peeled and deveined
- 2 tbsp Cajun seasoning
- Corn or flour tortillas
- **Remoulade Sauce:**
    - 1/2 cup mayonnaise
    - 1 tbsp Dijon mustard
    - 1 tbsp lemon juice
    - 1 tbsp chopped pickles
    - Salt and pepper to taste

Instructions:

1. Toss shrimp with Cajun seasoning. Sauté in a skillet over medium heat until cooked through (about 3-4 minutes).
2. In a bowl, mix all remoulade ingredients until well combined.
3. Warm the tortillas and fill with Cajun shrimp. Top with remoulade and serve warm.

Tex-Mex Breakfast Tacos with Chorizo

Ingredients:

- 1 lb chorizo, cooked and crumbled
- 4 eggs, scrambled
- Corn or flour tortillas
- Toppings: shredded cheese, diced tomatoes, avocado

Instructions:

1. In a skillet, cook chorizo until browned. Add scrambled eggs and cook until set.
2. Warm the tortillas and fill with chorizo and egg mixture.
3. Top with shredded cheese, diced tomatoes, and avocado. Serve warm.

German Bratwurst Tacos with Sauerkraut

Ingredients:

- 4 bratwurst sausages, cooked and sliced
- Corn or flour tortillas
- 1 cup sauerkraut
- Toppings: spicy mustard, chopped parsley

Instructions:

1. Warm the tortillas and fill with sliced bratwurst.
2. Top with sauerkraut, spicy mustard, and chopped parsley. Serve warm.

Ramen Noodle Tacos with Pork Belly

Ingredients:

- 1 lb pork belly, cooked and sliced
- 2 cups cooked ramen noodles
- Corn or flour tortillas
- Toppings: green onions, sesame seeds, pickled ginger

Instructions:

1. Warm the tortillas and fill with sliced pork belly and cooked ramen noodles.
2. Top with green onions, sesame seeds, and pickled ginger. Serve warm.

Spanish Chorizo and Egg Tacos

Ingredients:

- 1 lb Spanish chorizo, cooked and crumbled
- 4 eggs, scrambled
- Corn or flour tortillas
- Toppings: fresh cilantro, avocado slices

Instructions:

1. In a skillet, cook chorizo until browned. Add scrambled eggs and cook until set.
2. Warm the tortillas and fill with chorizo and egg mixture.
3. Top with fresh cilantro and avocado slices. Serve warm.

Pesto Chicken Tacos with Mozzarella

Ingredients:

- 1 lb cooked chicken, shredded
- 1/2 cup pesto
- Corn or flour tortillas
- Toppings: fresh mozzarella balls, cherry tomatoes

Instructions:

1. In a bowl, mix shredded chicken with pesto.
2. Warm the tortillas and fill with pesto chicken.
3. Top with fresh mozzarella balls and halved cherry tomatoes. Serve warm.

Crab and Avocado Tacos with Cilantro Lime Dressing

Ingredients:

- 1 lb cooked crab meat
- 1 avocado, diced
- Corn or flour tortillas
- **Cilantro Lime Dressing:**
    - 1/2 cup mayonnaise
    - 1/4 cup cilantro
    - Juice of 1 lime
    - Salt and pepper to taste

Instructions:

1. In a bowl, combine mayonnaise, cilantro, lime juice, salt, and pepper to make the dressing.
2. Warm the tortillas and fill with crab meat and diced avocado.
3. Drizzle with cilantro lime dressing and serve warm.

Filipino Adobo Chicken Tacos

Ingredients:

- 1 lb chicken thighs, cooked and shredded
- 1/2 cup adobo sauce (soy sauce, vinegar, garlic, bay leaves)
- Corn or flour tortillas
- Toppings: sliced green onions, chopped cilantro

Instructions:

1. In a bowl, mix shredded chicken with adobo sauce until well coated.
2. Warm the tortillas and fill with adobo chicken.
3. Top with sliced green onions and chopped cilantro. Serve warm.

Vegan Jackfruit Tacos with Mango Salsa

Ingredients:

- 1 can young green jackfruit, drained and shredded
- 1 tbsp olive oil
- 1 tsp smoked paprika
- 1 tsp cumin
- Corn or flour tortillas
- **Mango Salsa:**
    - 1 ripe mango, diced
    - 1/4 red onion, diced
    - 1 jalapeño, seeded and diced
    - Juice of 1 lime
    - Salt to taste

Instructions:

1. In a skillet, heat olive oil over medium heat. Add shredded jackfruit, smoked paprika, and cumin, cooking for about 10 minutes until softened.
2. In a bowl, combine mango, red onion, jalapeño, lime juice, and salt for the salsa.
3. Warm the tortillas, fill with jackfruit, and top with mango salsa. Serve warm.

Swedish Meatball Tacos with Lingonberry Sauce

Ingredients:

- 1 lb ground beef or turkey
- 1/2 cup breadcrumbs
- 1/4 cup onion, finely chopped
- 1 egg
- Salt and pepper to taste
- Corn or flour tortillas
- **Lingonberry Sauce:**
    - 1 cup lingonberry preserves

Instructions:

1. In a bowl, mix ground meat, breadcrumbs, onion, egg, salt, and pepper. Form into small meatballs.
2. Cook meatballs in a skillet over medium heat until browned and cooked through (about 10-12 minutes).
3. Warm the tortillas, fill with meatballs, and drizzle with lingonberry sauce. Serve warm.

Szechuan Beef Tacos with Cabbage Slaw

Ingredients:

- 1 lb ground beef
- 2 tbsp Szechuan sauce
- Corn or flour tortillas
- **Cabbage Slaw:**
    - 2 cups shredded cabbage
    - 1/4 cup carrots, shredded
    - 1 tbsp rice vinegar
    - 1 tsp sesame oil

Instructions:

1. In a skillet, cook ground beef until browned. Stir in Szechuan sauce and heat through.
2. In a bowl, combine cabbage, carrots, rice vinegar, and sesame oil for the slaw.
3. Warm the tortillas, fill with Szechuan beef, and top with cabbage slaw. Serve warm.

Cilantro Lime Grilled Shrimp Tacos

Ingredients:

- 1 lb shrimp, peeled and deveined
- 2 tbsp olive oil
- Juice of 1 lime
- 1/4 cup chopped cilantro
- Corn or flour tortillas
- Toppings: diced avocado, lime wedges

Instructions:

1. In a bowl, mix shrimp with olive oil, lime juice, and cilantro. Marinate for 15 minutes.
2. Grill shrimp on medium-high heat for 2-3 minutes per side until cooked through.
3. Warm the tortillas, fill with grilled shrimp, and top with diced avocado. Serve with lime wedges.

Smoked Salmon Tacos with Cream Cheese and Capers

Ingredients:

- 8 oz smoked salmon
- Corn or flour tortillas
- 1/2 cup cream cheese
- 1/4 cup capers
- Toppings: sliced red onion, dill

Instructions:

1. Warm the tortillas. Spread cream cheese on each tortilla.
2. Layer smoked salmon on top, adding capers and sliced red onion.
3. Garnish with fresh dill and serve.

Eggplant Parmesan Tacos

Ingredients:

- 1 medium eggplant, sliced
- 1 cup breadcrumbs
- 1 cup marinara sauce
- 1 cup mozzarella cheese, shredded
- Corn or flour tortillas
- Toppings: fresh basil

Instructions:

1. Preheat oven to 375°F (190°C). Dip eggplant slices in breadcrumbs and place on a baking sheet. Bake for 25 minutes until golden brown.
2. In a skillet, heat marinara sauce. Add baked eggplant and top with mozzarella cheese until melted.
3. Warm the tortillas, fill with eggplant mixture, and garnish with fresh basil. Serve warm.

Maple Glazed Salmon Tacos with Slaw

Ingredients:

- 1 lb salmon fillets
- 1/4 cup maple syrup
- 2 tbsp soy sauce
- Corn or flour tortillas
- **Slaw:**
    - 2 cups cabbage, shredded
    - 1/4 cup carrots, shredded
    - 2 tbsp apple cider vinegar

Instructions:

1. Preheat oven to 400°F (200°C). In a small bowl, mix maple syrup and soy sauce. Brush over salmon fillets.
2. Bake salmon for 12-15 minutes until cooked through.
3. In a bowl, mix cabbage, carrots, and vinegar for the slaw.
4. Warm the tortillas, fill with salmon, and top with slaw. Serve warm.

Coconut Curry Chicken Tacos

Ingredients:

- 1 lb cooked chicken, shredded
- 1 cup coconut milk
- 2 tbsp red curry paste
- Corn or flour tortillas
- Toppings: sliced green onions, cilantro

Instructions:

1. In a skillet, combine shredded chicken, coconut milk, and red curry paste. Simmer for 10 minutes.
2. Warm the tortillas, fill with coconut curry chicken, and top with green onions and cilantro. Serve warm.

Thai Red Curry Shrimp Tacos

Ingredients:

- 1 lb shrimp, peeled and deveined
- 1 cup coconut milk
- 2 tbsp red curry paste
- Corn or flour tortillas
- Toppings: sliced cucumber, lime wedges

Instructions:

1. In a skillet, combine shrimp, coconut milk, and red curry paste. Cook until shrimp is pink and cooked through (about 4-5 minutes).
2. Warm the tortillas, fill with Thai red curry shrimp, and top with sliced cucumber. Serve with lime wedges.

Chili Lime Mango Chicken Tacos

Ingredients:

- 1 lb chicken breast, diced
- 1 tbsp olive oil
- Juice of 2 limes
- 1 tsp chili powder
- 1 ripe mango, diced
- Corn or flour tortillas
- Toppings: diced red onion, cilantro

Instructions:

1. In a bowl, combine chicken, olive oil, lime juice, and chili powder. Marinate for 15-30 minutes.
2. Cook marinated chicken in a skillet over medium heat until fully cooked (about 7-10 minutes).
3. Warm the tortillas, fill with chicken, and top with diced mango, red onion, and cilantro. Serve warm.

Ratatouille Veggie Tacos

Ingredients:

- 1 zucchini, diced
- 1 eggplant, diced
- 1 bell pepper, diced
- 1 onion, diced
- 2 cups diced tomatoes (canned or fresh)
- 1 tbsp olive oil
- Corn or flour tortillas
- Toppings: fresh basil, feta cheese

Instructions:

1. In a skillet, heat olive oil over medium heat. Sauté onion, bell pepper, zucchini, and eggplant until tender (about 8-10 minutes).
2. Add diced tomatoes and simmer for 5-7 minutes.
3. Warm the tortillas, fill with ratatouille, and top with fresh basil and feta cheese. Serve warm.

Buffalo Chicken Tacos with Ranch Dressing

Ingredients:

- 1 lb shredded cooked chicken
- 1/2 cup buffalo sauce
- Corn or flour tortillas
- **Ranch Dressing:**
    - 1/2 cup plain Greek yogurt
    - 1 tbsp ranch seasoning

Instructions:

1. In a bowl, mix shredded chicken with buffalo sauce until well coated.
2. In another bowl, combine Greek yogurt and ranch seasoning for the dressing.
3. Warm the tortillas, fill with buffalo chicken, and drizzle with ranch dressing. Serve warm.

Tandoori Chicken Tacos with Mint Yogurt

Ingredients:

- 1 lb chicken thighs, diced
- 2 tbsp tandoori spice mix
- 1/2 cup plain yogurt
- 1/4 cup fresh mint, chopped
- Corn or flour tortillas
- Toppings: sliced cucumbers, lettuce

Instructions:

1. In a bowl, mix diced chicken with tandoori spice and let marinate for at least 30 minutes.
2. In another bowl, combine yogurt and chopped mint for the mint yogurt.
3. Cook marinated chicken in a skillet over medium heat until fully cooked (about 7-10 minutes).
4. Warm the tortillas, fill with chicken, and top with mint yogurt, sliced cucumbers, and lettuce. Serve warm.

Fajita-style Beef Tacos with Chimichurri

Ingredients:

- 1 lb flank steak, sliced
- 1 bell pepper, sliced
- 1 onion, sliced
- 1 tbsp olive oil
- **Chimichurri:**
    - 1/2 cup fresh parsley, chopped
    - 2 tbsp red wine vinegar
    - 1/4 cup olive oil
    - 2 garlic cloves, minced

Instructions:

1. In a bowl, mix parsley, red wine vinegar, olive oil, and garlic to make chimichurri.
2. In a skillet, heat olive oil and sauté sliced beef, bell pepper, and onion until cooked to your liking (about 5-7 minutes).
3. Warm the tortillas, fill with beef and veggies, and drizzle with chimichurri. Serve warm.

Lemon Herb Grilled Chicken Tacos

Ingredients:

- 1 lb chicken breast, diced
- 2 tbsp olive oil
- Juice of 1 lemon
- 1 tbsp dried herbs (oregano, thyme, or rosemary)
- Corn or flour tortillas
- Toppings: avocado slices, cilantro

Instructions:

1. In a bowl, combine chicken, olive oil, lemon juice, and dried herbs. Marinate for at least 30 minutes.
2. Grill marinated chicken until cooked through (about 7-10 minutes).
3. Warm the tortillas, fill with grilled chicken, and top with avocado slices and cilantro. Serve warm.

Sriracha Tofu Tacos with Sesame Slaw

Ingredients:

- 1 block firm tofu, pressed and cubed
- 2 tbsp sriracha sauce
- 1 tbsp soy sauce
- Corn or flour tortillas
- **Sesame Slaw:**
    - 2 cups cabbage, shredded
    - 1/4 cup carrots, shredded
    - 1 tbsp sesame oil
    - 1 tbsp rice vinegar

Instructions:

1. In a bowl, mix tofu, sriracha, and soy sauce. Let marinate for 15-30 minutes.
2. In a skillet, cook marinated tofu until crispy (about 10-12 minutes).
3. In another bowl, mix cabbage, carrots, sesame oil, and rice vinegar for the slaw.
4. Warm the tortillas, fill with tofu, and top with sesame slaw. Serve warm.

Curried Beef Tacos with Raita

Ingredients:

- 1 lb ground beef
- 2 tbsp curry powder
- Corn or flour tortillas
- **Raita:**
    - 1 cup plain yogurt
    - 1/4 cucumber, diced
    - 1/4 tsp cumin

Instructions:

1. In a skillet, cook ground beef until browned. Stir in curry powder and cook for another 2 minutes.
2. In another bowl, mix yogurt, diced cucumber, and cumin for the raita.
3. Warm the tortillas, fill with curried beef, and top with raita. Serve warm.

Cilantro Lime Pork Tacos with Avocado

Ingredients:

- 1 lb pork tenderloin, diced
- 2 tbsp olive oil
- Juice and zest of 2 limes
- 1/4 cup fresh cilantro, chopped
- Corn or flour tortillas
- Toppings: sliced avocado, diced onion

Instructions:

1. In a bowl, combine diced pork, olive oil, lime juice, lime zest, and cilantro. Marinate for at least 30 minutes.
2. Cook marinated pork in a skillet over medium heat until fully cooked (about 10-12 minutes).
3. Warm the tortillas, fill with pork, and top with sliced avocado and diced onion. Serve warm.

Grilled Veggie Tacos with Balsamic Glaze

Ingredients:

- 1 zucchini, sliced
- 1 bell pepper, sliced
- 1 red onion, sliced
- 2 tbsp olive oil
- 1/4 cup balsamic glaze
- Corn or flour tortillas
- Toppings: fresh basil or parsley

Instructions:

1. Preheat the grill. In a bowl, toss vegetables with olive oil and a pinch of salt.
2. Grill the vegetables until tender and slightly charred (about 5-7 minutes).
3. Drizzle with balsamic glaze after grilling.
4. Warm the tortillas, fill with grilled veggies, and top with fresh herbs. Serve warm.

Egg and Bacon Breakfast Tacos

Ingredients:

- 4 eggs
- 4 slices of bacon, cooked and crumbled
- Corn or flour tortillas
- Toppings: shredded cheese, diced tomatoes, and avocado

Instructions:

1. Scramble the eggs in a skillet over medium heat until cooked through.
2. Warm the tortillas and fill them with scrambled eggs, crumbled bacon, and desired toppings. Serve warm.

Spicy Tuna Poke Tacos

Ingredients:

- 1 lb sushi-grade tuna, diced
- 2 tbsp soy sauce
- 1 tbsp sriracha (or to taste)
- Corn or flour tortillas
- Toppings: diced avocado, cucumber, and sesame seeds

Instructions:

1. In a bowl, combine diced tuna, soy sauce, and sriracha. Toss to coat.
2. Warm the tortillas, fill with spicy tuna, and top with avocado, cucumber, and sesame seeds. Serve chilled.

Roasted Vegetable Tacos with Hummus

Ingredients:

- 1 bell pepper, diced
- 1 zucchini, diced
- 1 red onion, diced
- 2 tbsp olive oil
- 1 cup hummus
- Corn or flour tortillas
- Toppings: fresh cilantro

Instructions:

1. Preheat the oven to 400°F (200°C). Toss vegetables with olive oil and roast for 20-25 minutes until tender.
2. Warm the tortillas, spread hummus inside, fill with roasted vegetables, and top with fresh cilantro. Serve warm.

Balsamic Chicken Tacos with Goat Cheese

Ingredients:

- 1 lb chicken breast, diced
- 2 tbsp balsamic vinegar
- 2 tbsp olive oil
- 4 oz goat cheese, crumbled
- Corn or flour tortillas
- Toppings: arugula or spinach

Instructions:

1. In a bowl, combine chicken, balsamic vinegar, and olive oil. Marinate for 30 minutes.
2. Cook marinated chicken in a skillet over medium heat until fully cooked (about 7-10 minutes).
3. Warm the tortillas, fill with chicken, top with crumbled goat cheese and arugula. Serve warm.

Lobster Tacos with Cilantro and Lime

Ingredients:

- 1 lb cooked lobster meat, chopped
- Juice of 1 lime
- 2 tbsp fresh cilantro, chopped
- Corn or flour tortillas
- Toppings: diced tomatoes and avocado

Instructions:

1. In a bowl, combine chopped lobster meat, lime juice, and cilantro.
2. Warm the tortillas, fill with lobster mixture, and top with diced tomatoes and avocado. Serve chilled or slightly warm.